new.u

Jason Creech

Innovo
Publishing

Published by
Innovo Publishing, LLC
www.innovopublishing.com
1-888-546-2111

Innovo
Publishing

Providing Full-Service Publishing Services for
Christian Authors, Artists & Organizations: Hardbacks, Paperbacks,
eBooks, Audiobooks, Music & Videos

All Scripture quotations, unless otherwise indicated, are taken from the Holy Bible:
New King James Version (NKJV) Copyright 1982, New Spirit-Filled Life Bible,
Copyright 2002 by Thomas Nelson, Inc.

Library of Congress Control Number: 2011935940
ISBN 13: 978-1-936076-64-2
ISBN 10: 1-936076-64-0

Cover Design & Interior Layout: Innovo Publishing, LLC

Printed in the United States of America
U.S. Printing History

Second Edition: August 2011

week 1
belief / eliminating every doubt

DAY 1: **TRUE OR FALSE?**

Some time ago, I was standing in aisle nine waiting to check out at our local Walmart. Judging by the ridiculous wait, I suppose word leaked out that the world was coming to an end and everyone rushed to Wally World one last time. Every lane was jam packed, nothing was moving, and no one was happy. As I scanned over the tabloids, I noticed a monthly publication called *Weekly World News*. Their slogan was what intrigued me the most: "The World's Only Reliable Newspaper." Below their slogan were the words, "All new—shocking—bizarre—incredible—and it's all true." Allow me to share with you a few article titles listed in this "World's Only Reliable Newspaper." Keep in mind, they're all true!

- Einstein's brain came to life and went on a rampage
- Drunk ghost ruins his own funeral
- Survivors recently discovered on the *Titanic*
- Tornado helps family move (This one might be true.)
- Scientists say that hurricanes can now be stopped by poking the eye of the storm
- Seven-year-old boy grows a full beard and mustache (I think he was in my second-grade homeroom.)

Now this got me to thinking, *What determines if something is true? Is something true simply because you believe it or because you read it somewhere? Is something true because your parents told you it was?* I jumped in my car and drove to a nearby library. I told the librarian I was battling with something I had been taught my entire life, and I needed something or someone to validate what I had been taught. She was reluctant, but she offered to help. "What are you questioning?" she asked. I don't know what she was expecting to hear but my question was, "Who was the first president of the United States of America?" That poor lady thought I had lost my mind. She looked at me and said, "Sir, that would be George Washington. Trust me; it's true. It's in the book!" I'm sure this sounds kind of lame, but think about all the stuff we believe to be true, simply because we grew up hearing it and reading it.

Let's go down this road for a minute. Pretend you and I attend two different elementary schools with two different history teachers who teach from two different history books. Now let's say that your teacher and your book say George Washington was the first president of the United States. However, my teacher and my book say James Monroe was the first president of the United States. Who's right? How do we know who is telling the truth?

Here's my point . . .

I grew up in the Bible Belt—where there's a church on every corner. I've heard enough sermons to last me a thousand lifetimes. But at one point in my life, I started to question. I started to wonder if what I had been taught was true or not. During a deep discussion with a friend, he asked the question, "Can't all religions be right?" Then it dawned on me; the answer is obvious—no, they can't! Each faith teaches something totally different. Buddhists believe there is no god, Jews believe in one god, and Hindus believe in many gods. As Stephen Prothero writes: "The world's religious rivals do converge when it comes to ethics, but they diverge sharply on doctrine, ritual, mythology, experience, and law."[1] Each has their unique belief about the beginning and ending of our world, heaven, hell, salvation, and a slew of other core topics. Since one contradicts the other, the only possibilities are:

1. They're all wrong;

    or

2. One is right and the others are wrong.

They can all be wrong or one can be right and the others wrong, but one thing is absolutely, positively certain—they cannot all be right. No way! No how!

DOSE OF TRUTH

"And you shall know the truth, and the truth shall make you free."
— John 8:32

"However, when He, the Spirit of truth, has come, He will guide you into all truth; for He will not speak on His own authority, but whatever He hears He will speak; and He will tell you things to come." — **John 16:13**

MAKIN' IT REAL

Make a list of things you believed in as a child—things you later discovered not to be true.

Did your discovery of those things affect the way you view God? If so, take a few minutes to elaborate.

DAY 2: WHY SHOULD I BELIEVE CREATION OVER EVOLUTION?

I was probably somewhere around eight or nine years old when I had my first serious God-thought struggle. My mom and I were having a deep, theological God-talk. The discussion started when I asked, "How old is God? What's His mom and dad's name? What planet was He born on?" When my mom told me God was eternal and that He had always been, I was totally confused. How could something or someone have no beginning? It's this same thought that drives many people away from the faith. But when you think about it, we really only have three options:

1. **God is eternal. He created everything.** He has no beginning so He needs no creator, nothing to ignite His existence. If that's not the case, then we have to consider the second possibility.

2. **There is no God. The universe is eternal, it has no beginning, and it is the product of evolution.** Now here's my question, "Why can the universe be eternal and God not be?" Whether you say God is eternal or the universe is eternal, either way you're saying you believe there is an eternity and someone or something exists within it. However, one must keep in mind that science itself does not cling to the idea of an eternal universe. That brings us to a third option . . .

3. **There is no God and the universe has a beginning, thus the Big Bang Theory.** But is this really an option? What created the Bang? What existed before the Bang occurred? What began the Bang? Everything that has a beginning, has a beginner.

Science is the search for truth. Truth can be established by factual evidence, but something can be true long before there's a known fact to support it. The question to be asked is, "Where do the facts fall?" During the twentieth century, experts in the field of science discovered that the universe is growing. The Hubble Space Telescope taught us that the universe is rapidly expanding the same in all directions. So if the universe is expanding in all directions, it had to have started at some point. If we could rewind time far enough, we would find the birth of our universe. Since the 1920s, scientists have called this starting point The Big Bang, and almost every scientist today adheres to this idea.

During the mid-1800s, a man by the name of Charles Darwin said that all living things evolved from one common ancestor. His teachings completely changed the study of science. Darwin claimed that all life began with a single-celled organism that morphed over a long period of time, leaving us with every form of life today. All science would need to validate Darwin's theory is the discovery of one fossil to support the idea. But that's yet to be the case. Granted, there's been a few that were esteemed as the "missing link"; however, not one has avoided intense scrutiny—if not completely dismissed from the list of possibilities. Actually, science has taught us that if we started beneath the earth's crust and worked our way to the surface, we would find very little fossilized forms until we came to a certain point. At that spot there is an explosion of fossilized life forms—fossils of many complex species. Creatures of all kinds left their stamp within the earth's rocky surface. This discovery is called the Cambrian Explosion. Embedded in the rock of this earth is the evidence that supports the Bible's account of creation. No wonder Jesus said, "If they don't praise Me, the rocks will cry out" (**Luke 19:40**).

DOSE OF TRUTH

"All things were created through Him and for Him. And He is before all things, and in Him all things consist." — **Colossians 1:16–17**

"You laid the foundations of the earth, and the heavens are the work of Your hands." — **Psalm 102:25**

MAKIN' IT REAL

Do you think Christians are viewed as intelligent, educated thinkers or are most Christians perceived to be simple and unlearned? Take a minute to explain your answer.

Can science and faith go hand in hand? Why or why not?

What's the first God-thought struggle you've ever had?

How has today's devotion affected your outlook on the creation?

DAY 3: **THE BIG GOD QUESTION**

Perhaps the greatest God question of all time is this: "If there's a God, why is there so much suffering throughout the world?" It's a great question, I do agree. We are told that on our little planet, over 25,000 children die of starvation every day. According to a recent study released by Procter & Gamble, 58 percent of the world's population lives off less than $1,500 a year. With all the war, famine, natural disasters, disease, etc., it's easy to question the idea of a loving God. I once sat with a young teenage girl not long after she had been raped by a much older cousin. Words cannot describe the depth of anger churning inside that broken young lady. Although she claimed to be an atheist, she repeatedly cursed God. After letting her vent for a while, I gently leaned toward her and asked, "If you could say anything to God, anything at all, what would it be?" She lifted her head and looked me right in the eyes. With big tears falling off her cheeks she asked, "If You are real, and You knew this would happen to me, why did You create me? Why?" In the middle of so much heartache, can we hang our hopes on a loving Creator?

Where is God in all the mess?

To answer the question, let's consider what the Bible says in **Psalm 115:16**. The writer says, "The heaven, even the heavens, are the Lord's; but the earth He has given to the children of men." Is there a loving God? Yes! Why all the suffering? Because our loving God gave us this world and this is what we've done with the gift we received.

In the book of Genesis, we find God gave Adam dominion over the earth. We've been given the power to shape our world for good or evil, for better or worse. God created us and granted us the freedom to do whatever we please. If we want war, we can have it. If we want addiction, we can have it. If we want to destroy our family, we can go for it. We're that free. But when you suffer, know this; He suffers too. When you cry, remember this; He cries too. As a matter of fact, **Hebrews 2:18** says Jesus suffered so that He can help us during our time of suffering. Can a loving God exist in the middle of our mess? You bet! Not only can He exist, He can also assist.

DOSE OF TRUTH

"For You have made him a little lower than the angels, and You have crowned him with glory and honor. You have made him to have dominion over the works of Your hands; you have put all *things* under his feet, all sheep and oxen—even the beasts of the field." — **Psalm 8:5–7**

MAKIN' IT REAL

What are some things in your life that have caused you to question God?

Have you had an honest talk with God about those things? Have you shared with Him your disappointments and frustrations? He encourages us to cast our cares on Him so if you haven't, take a few minutes and do it now.

DAY 4: **CAN THE BIBLE BE TRUSTED?**

The Bible is comprised of sixty-six books, or letters, originally written from three different languages, over a period of 1,500 years, and written by forty different authors. Many kingdoms have sought its destruction, yet it is still the bestselling book of the world today. On one hand, the Bible is a historical book that is backed by archeology; on the other hand, it's a prophetic book that has lived up to all of its claims thus far. But many have wondered if the Bible has been accurately passed down. How true is it to what it was in the beginning? Imagine, for example, someone adding or taking away from the Ten Commandments or eliminating the Book of Acts from The New Testament. Imagine a person's adding to or twisting around the things Jesus said or did.

You see, many ancient writings adhered only loosely to the facts of the events they reported. Some highly regarded authors of the ancient world, for example, reported events that took place many years before they were born . . . in countries they had never visited! And while their writing may be largely factual, historians admit that greater credibility must be granted to writers who were both geographically and chronologically close to the events they reported. With that in mind, look at the loving care God took when He inspired the writing of the New Testament. The overwhelming weight of scholarship confirms that the accounts of Jesus' life, the history of the early church, and the letters that form the bulk of the New Testament were all written by men who were either eyewitnesses of the events they recorded or contemporaries of eyewitnesses. The writer John said, "We are telling you about what we ourselves have actually seen and heard" (**1 John 1:3**).

Historians evaluate the textual reliability of ancient literature according to two standards:

1. What is the time interval between the original and the earliest copy?
2. How many manuscripts are available?

So, for example, virtually everything we know today about Julius Caesar's exploits in the Gallic Wars is derived from ten manuscript copies, the earliest of which dates to within 1,000 years of the time the Gallic Wars were written. By comparison, the text of Homer's *The Iliad* is much more reliable. It is supported by 643 manuscript copies in existence today, with a mere 400-year gap between the date of composition. Using this same standard to compare the validity of the New Testament, we must say that there is no comparison to the Holy Scriptures. It has no equal. Nearly 25,000 manuscripts of the New Testament reside in libraries and universities of the world today. The earliest of these is a fragment of John's gospel currently located in the John Rylands Library of Manchester, England; it has been dated to within fifty years of the date when the apostle John penned the original.[2]

DOSE OF TRUTH

"I assure you, until heaven and earth disappear, even the smallest detail of God's law will remain until its purpose is achieved." **— Matthew 5:18**

MAKIN' IT REAL

Why do you think the Bible is the center of so much debate?

DAY 5: WHY SHOULD I BELIEVE JESUS WAS WHO HE SAID HE WAS?

In late August of 2006, every news media across the U.S. featured the story of two men taken hostage by Islamic extremists during the War on Terrorism. A Palestinian news agency released a video reporting the capture of Fox News correspondent, Steve Centanni, and New Zealand cameraman, Olaf Wiig. Olaf tells the story in a CNN interview: "We are summoned into this room, where there's a guy sitting with and a saber on the floor. And you just think, *This is the end*." Olaf was asked a blunt, point-blank question . . . it was certainly not a question he was expecting. His captor asked, "Who was Jesus?" On the twenty-third day of August, the two men, exhausted but alive, issued their own appeal. Their captors demanded that all Muslim prisoners be released from U.S. jails. But just three days later, there was another video, showing Olaf and Steve, saying they'd converted to Islam. They were free within two hours. Olaf said his conversion came at the point of a gun.

So how would you answer the question?

Who was Jesus?

The book of Acts is a historical recording of Christianity and its conception. Repeatedly we read where believers proved that Jesus was indeed the Messiah, God's Son. They did this by referring to the prophetic Scriptures listed throughout the Old Testament. We see this in **Acts 9:22**, **Acts 18:28**, **Acts 3:23–24**, **Acts 7:51–53**, **Acts 10:39–43**, **Acts 13:27–31**, **Acts 17:2–3**, **Acts 17:11**, **Acts 24:14**, and **Acts 26:22**. In **Romans 16:25–26**, the Bible says that we are established by our knowledge of the prophetic Scriptures given to all nations. Jesus also spoke of these Old Testament prophecies saying, "These are the words which I spoke to you while I was still with you, that all things must be fulfilled which were written in the Law of Moses" (**Luke 24:44–45**). So why are the Old Testament prophecies such a big deal? First of all, these are very detailed prophecies. As a matter of fact, there are over 300 detailed prophecies listed in the Old Testament! According to the science of statistics and probabilities, the chances of one man fulfilling only eight of the Old Testament prophecies is 100 quadrillion to 1. For years, atheists believed that the church added the prophecies into the Old Testament to make the life and death of Jesus agree with the text. However, in 1956, the Dead Sea Scrolls were discovered. That discovery completely busted the myth. After extensive testing, the Dead Sea Scrolls were dated between 200–250 BC (Before Christ)! We now have copies from the Old Testament containing over 300 prophecies and these copies were written more than 200 years before Christ was even born! Just like the Roman solider at the cross, we too must look at Jesus and say, "Surely this must have been the Son of God."

DOSE OF TRUTH

Pilate therefore said to Him, "Are You a king then?" Jesus answered, "You say *rightly* that I am a king. For this cause I was born, and for this cause I have come into the world, that I should bear witness to the truth. Everyone who is of the truth hears My voice." Pilate said to Him, "What is truth?" — **John 18:37–38**

Jesus said to him, "I am the way, the truth, and the life. No one comes to the Father except through Me." — **John 14:6**

MAKIN' IT REAL

Based on today's devotion, what do you think the first-century believers were like?

How might typical believers then, differ from typical believers now?

DAY 6: **WHAT ARE THE ODDS?**

One hundred quadrillion to one—that's the odds of one man fulfilling only eight of the detailed prophecies contained within the Old Testament. Let's consider what 100 quadrillion looks like. As Josh McDowell put it in his book, *Beyond Belief*:

> Look at it this way; if you were to take 100,000,000,000,000,000 (100 quadrillion) silver dollars and spread them across the state of Texas, they would not only cover the entire state but also form a pile of coins two feet deep. Now, take one more silver dollar, mark it with a big red X, toss it into the pile, and stir the whole pile thoroughly. Then, blindfold yourself, and starting at El Paso on the western border of the state, walk the length and breadth of that enormous state, stooping just once along the way to pick up a single silver dollar. Then take off your blindfold, and look at the silver dollar in your hand. What are the chances that you would pick the marked coin out of a pile? The same chance that one person could have fulfilled just eight messianic prophecies in one lifetime.

We're not talking about vague words that one could easily live their life around either. These are extremely detailed predictions that point us toward Jesus. Imagine this with me . . . Let's say that you and I met through an email or a written letter, before the days of Facebook and other forms of social media. For months, we sent messages back and forth. Then one day we decided to meet. How would we arrange our first meeting? Of course, we would pick a place and choose a day and time. But I would also go beyond that. I would tell you the kind of car I will be driving, the color of the car, what I would be wearing, the color of my hair, my height, and MAYBE my weight. I would give you every detail I could, in hopes that you would know me when I arrive. That's exactly what Jesus did. Notice the detailed list of prophecies listed below along with the reference of their fulfillment. Have no doubts; Jesus is everything He claimed to be.

- He will be betrayed by a friend (**Psalm 41:9; Matthew 26:49**).
- He would be betrayed for thirty pieces of silver (**Zechariah 11:12; Matthew 26:15**).
- His betrayal money will be cast to the floor of My temple (**Zechariah 11:13; Matthew 27:5**).
- His betrayal money will be used to buy the potter's field (**Zechariah 11:13; Matthew 27:7**).
- He will be forsaken and deserted by His disciples (**Zechariah 13:7; Mark 14:50**).
- He will be accused by false witnesses (**Psalm 35:11; Matthew 26:59–60**).
- He will be wounded and bruised (**Isaiah 53:5; Matthew 27:26**).
- He will be stuck and spit upon (**Isaiah 50:6; Matthew 26:67**).
- He will be executed among sinners (**Isaiah 53:12; Matthew 37:38**).
- His hands and feet will be pierced (**Psalm 22:16; Luke 23:33**).
- He will pray for His persecutors (**Isaiah 53:12; Luke 23:34**).
- His friends and family will stand afar off and watch (**Psalm 38:11; Luke 23:49**).
- His garments will be divided and won by the casting of lots (**Psalm 22:18; John 19:23–24**).
- He will be given gall and vinegar (**Psalm 69:21; Matthew 27:34**).
- His bones will be left unbroken (**Psalm 34:20; John 19:33**).
- His heart would rupture (**Psalm 22:14; John 19:34**).
- His side will be pierced (**Zechariah 12:10; John 19:34**).
- Darkness will come over the land at midday (**Amos 8:9; Matthew 27:45**).
- He will be buried in a rich man's tomb (**Isaiah 53:9; Matthew 27:57–60**).
- He will die 483 years after the declaration of Artaxerxes to rebuild the temple in 444 BC (**Daniel 9:24**).[3]

Surely, Jesus was who He said He was.

DOSE OF TRUTH

"Always be prepared to give an answer to everyone who asks you to give the reason for the hope that you have." — **1 Peter 3:15**

MAKIN' IT REAL

How does the last two days' devotion assure your faith in Jesus?

If someone asked you to explain why you believe in the deity of Christ, how would you respond?

DAY 7: **THE CHANGE IN ME**

On March 15, 1992, I met Jesus Christ in a personal way and that meeting wrecked me for life—in the greatest of ways, that is! For some time, I had been going to church off and on with my mom. While the worship team led the congregation, I would watch how people responded; the level of joy in that auditorium was amazing. Some wept tears of joy while others grinned ear to ear as they sang along. The audience seemed to be clothed in a garment of peace that I knew nothing about. Without a doubt, those people had something my life was lacking. Peace was not something I was accustomed to. Externally my life was great. I had a wonderful family, caring parents, a younger brother, who I tormented daily (sorry Dustan), but internally I was a mess. Years of bad choices left me enslaved by sin and tormented by the bondage of addiction.

Sunday after Sunday I watched people during church. I began craving what they had. I wanted to know God the way those people knew God. Now several of my high-school friends came to church with their parents as well. We all filled a pew near the back of the sanctuary. The pastor made an invitation each week at the conclusion of service. He offered to pray with those who wanted to meet Jesus. I wasn't sure what that meant nor was I comfortable with all my friends watching me respond to the pastor's invitation. But soon the longing for freedom became more important than the opinion of those around me.

I responded.

Imagine trying to explain the taste of chocolate to someone who has never tasted chocolate before. It's even more challenging to express in words how sweet it is to experience Jesus. The Bible challenges us to, "Taste and see that the Lord is good." I can truly say without any doubt that I have tasted—and He is good! My life instantly began a major metamorphosis. Things that once enticed me, repulsed me. Even my school work reflected the difference Jesus made in me. In my freshman year of high school, I failed two classes for an entire semester. I became a Christian in March of my senior year. By the end of my freshman year of college, I was on the Dean's

List. Four years later, I earned my bachelor's degree, finishing college with a 3.4 GPA. What a difference Jesus made in my life!

Even my Christmas wish list had changed. The Christmas before I became a Christ follower, I asked for a set of chrome wheels for the 1978 Oldsmobile my uncle Buzz gave me. My parents always went out of their way to bless me and my brother. Needless to say, I got the wheels. I'm sure my mom and dad were shocked when I asked for the Bible on cassette the following year. A new hunger had captured my appetite. Like a junky, I wanted more. I ached for more of God's presence.

Why do I believe? Because I've tasted. I've experienced.

I know on a personal level that Jesus Christ is everything He claimed and claims to be, the Bible is God's Word, and my life is a living testimony of its authenticity.

DOSE OF TRUTH

Therefore, if anyone is in Christ, he is a new creation; old things have passed away; behold, all things have become new. — **2 Corinthians 5:17**

MAKIN' IT REAL

Name someone you know whose life has been radically changed because of their relationship with Jesus.

One of Satan's greatest lies is that we cannot change. Take a few minutes and identify the lies he has spoken to you over the years. Are there any areas in your life in which you are still allowing those lies to be a reality? If so, share those things with Jesus. Be honest! Know with confidence that He, and only He, can and will change us, free us, and make us a new creation.

week 2
confession / the journey begins

DAY 1: **GOOD FOLKS**

At this point, we've validated the credibility of a Creator, the authenticity of the Holy Bible, and the deity of Christ. So what's our Creator like? What does the Bible teach? And for what purpose did Jesus come? The Bible teaches us that God is love; however, He is also a just judge. **Hebrews 9:27** says that each of us has an appointment with death and after that comes the judgment. **Hebrews 10:31** says, "It is a fearful thing to fall into the hands of a living God." The Bible repeatedly addresses the fact that we have all sinned (**Romans 3:23** and **1 John 1:8–10**). Sin has its consequences and the ultimate consequence is death—physical death and spiritual death (**Romans 6:23**). Jesus came to save us from the punishment of sin. He took upon Himself the full judgment of our sin.

Over the next four weeks, I want to break this all down into small bite-sized pieces. My intentions are to simplify what can often become muddied by religious rhetoric and legalities. For now, let's start by defining sin.

Sin is every wrong thought that you've ever meditated on, every wrong word you've ever spoken, every wrong deed that you've ever done, every wrong feeling you've ever harbored, and the Bible says that every time you've had an opportunity to do good and didn't do it, that's sin. Wow! If all that is sin, how many times a day do you think the average person sins? It's a sobering thought, isn't it? Let's pretend that you and I are both really good folks, and being the nearly perfect people that we are, we only sin once a day. If you and I lived to be seventy years old, we would have committed 25,550 sins!

Now who would want to appear before a judge carrying a record book of 25,550 offenses? The frightening fact is, without a Savior, one day we will all do just that. **1 Peter 4:18** says, "If the righteous scarcely be saved, where will the ungodly and the sinner appear?"

DOSE OF TRUTH

Therefore, put to death your members which are on the earth: fornication, uncleanness, passion, evil desire, and covetousness, which is idolatry. Because of these things the wrath of God is coming upon the sons of disobedience, in which you yourselves once walked when you lived in them. But now you yourselves are to put off all these: anger, wrath, malice, blasphemy, filthy language out of your mouth. **— Colossians 3:5–8**

And the tongue is a fire, a world of iniquity. The tongue is so set among our members that it defiles the whole body, and sets on fire the course of nature; and it is set on fire by hell. **— James 3:6**

"But I say to you that for every idle word men may speak, they will give account of it in the day of judgment." **— Matthew 12:36**

"But if you do not forgive, neither will your Father in heaven forgive your trespasses." **— Mark 11:26**

And as it is appointed for men to die once, but after this the judgment. **— Hebrews 9:27**

Therefore, to him who knows to do good and does not do it, to him it is sin. **— James 4:17**

MAKIN' IT REAL

Have you ever done something wrong that you were majorly busted for? What was it? What happened?

When you do something wrong, do you act weird in any way? Sure you do; we all do, but why do we do this?

Do you think God sees everything we do?

One of the greatest lies of hell is that we can keep our secret sins a secret. Someone once said, "Anything you uncover, God will cover." But the flipside is also true. "Anything you cover, God will uncover." Deep down inside, we know that to be true, but for some reason we tend to ignore our secrets rather than deal with them. Why is that?

Do you think God loves you no matter what you've done?

DAY 2: **BUSTED**

Dewayne and I had been buddies for about a year I guess. His oldest brother had his own place on the other side of town. On the weekends, a bunch of my high-school friends would spend the night there. One night, I asked my mom if I could go. She was not fond of the idea and nothing I said would change her mind. So I thought I could trick her. Instead of going to Dewayne's brother's place, we would spend the night at his house. I assured her that both of his parents were home. She agreed and out the door I went. Later that night, she ran into Dewayne's mom at the grocery store. I'm sure you see where this is going. She asked if I was being a good guest. His mom was clueless. One question led to another, and I was caught. That next morning, as we drove home, there was a thick fog covering the valley where I lived. Off in the distance I spotted my mom. She was furious! That day, I discovered that my mom and Jackie Chan are first cousins. I also learned that you are never too old for a whippin'.

From the moment we were old enough to get into trouble, we've tried to hide our sins. Mark Twain said, "Every man is like the moon because we all hide a dark side." However, sin cannot be covered up. The Bible says that our hidden sins will find us out. Jesus said, "Everything done in secret will be proclaimed from the housetops." Proverbs says, "He who covers his sins shall not prosper." You see, God is aware of every deed that you've ever done.

One of my favorite stories is about a high-school girl and her new "pimped-out" sports car. Jamie got this new car one Thursday night, and Friday morning she picked up three of her friends before school. They skipped first period and cruised into the school parking lot as the bell rang to start the next class. The first person they ran into was Ms. Smith, their first-period teacher. Now, most of us would freak out about now, but these girls had a plan.

They told Ms. Smith that Jamie had a flat on the way to school and that's why they were late. Ms. Smith said, "Well, girls, you missed a test. However, if you hurry, I'm sure you can make the test up now; it's only a one-question test, and the question is very easy." The teacher set the girls in the four corners of the room and wrote this question on the board: "Which tire was flat?"

Busted!

DOSE OF TRUTH

. . . and be sure your sin will find you out. — **Numbers 32:23**

He who covers his sins will not prosper, but whoever confesses and forsakes them will have mercy. — **Proverbs 28:13**

"For there is nothing covered that will not be revealed, nor hidden that will not be known. Therefore, whatever you have spoken in the dark will be heard in the light, and what you have spoken in the ear in inner rooms will be proclaimed on the housetops." —**Luke 12:2–3**

Therefore, judge nothing before the time, until the Lord comes, who will both bring to light the hidden things of darkness and reveal the counsels of the hearts. Then each one's praise will come from God. — **1 Corinthians 4:5**

MAKIN' IT REAL

Do you think it's possible to keep something secret and never get nailed for it?

What's the longest period of time that you've gotten away with something?

Are you hiding something now, something you're ashamed of? Are you ready to deal with it?

What keeps you from taking it to Jesus?

Do you think He's ready to cover you with mercy?

Talk to Him about it. Today. Why not now?

DAY 3: **TWO KINDS OF PEOPLE**

Sin will be dealt with in one of two ways:

1.   Sin will be confessed and forgiven.

     Or

2.   Sin will be judged.

Let me explain it to you like this: Let's say that I'm driving my new Corvette through an intersection. Some knucklehead runs the red light and totals my new car. Obviously, the fella is guilty of breaking the law and destroying my car. Now imagine me pulling myself from the vehicle, walking over to this guilty man, and saying, "Don't worry about what happened. I forgive you." Now, that sounds great, but there's only one problem—someone has to pay for the damage that's been done!

This same situation applies to us spiritually. We sinned, and our sin created a debt that must be paid. **Romans 6:23** says, "The wages of sin is death." This death the Bible speaks of is physical death, spiritual death, and eternal death. You see, Christ didn't just forgive us for the sin we committed; He also paid for the damages. He died to pay off our debt. He took the wages of sin upon Himself.

C. S. Lewis once said that there are two types of people in the world. One group says to God, "Not my will, but Yours be done." The other group says to God, "Not Your will, but mine be done." Lewis said that one day, the second group will wake up in hell and hear God say to them, "Not My will, but yours be done." The Bible says that it's not God's will that any perish. As Max Lucado once wrote, "Jesus would rather go to hell for you than to go to heaven without you."

DOSE OF TRUTH

For the wages of sin is death, but the gift of God is eternal life in Christ Jesus our Lord. **—Romans 6:23**

The Lord is not slack concerning His promises, as some count slackness, but is longsuffering toward us, not willing that any should perish but that all should come to repentance. **—2 Peter 3:9**

"For God so loved the world that He gave His only begotten Son, that whoever believes in Him should not perish but have everlasting life. For God did not send His Son into the world to condemn the world, but that the world through Him might be saved. He who believes in Him is not condemned; but he who does not believe is condemned already, because he has not believed in the name of the only begotten Son of God. And this is the condemnation, that the light has come into the world, and men loved darkness rather than light, because their deeds were evil." **—John 3:16–19**

MAKIN' IT REAL

When you sin, how does that affect your time with God? Do you avoid God and other Christian people for long periods of time, or do you immediately run to God with your problem?

Why do you respond to your failure the way you do?

How do you think God wants you to respond to failure?

DAY 4: **POTTY MOUTH**

When my daughter was two years old, I was working for a church in Alabama. One morning, I got up before daybreak and found my way through the dark house. I had planned to have some early morning office hours. As I raised my toothbrush to my mouth, I noticed a nasty smell. Passing it off as extreme morning breath, I brushed my teeth for a few minutes and took off.

That afternoon, I came home for lunch and before I left the house, I took a few minutes to brush my teeth. As I started to brush, the smell hit me again. I pulled the toothbrush out of my mouth and took a whiff, and then I knelt down to my daughter's potty and took a whiff. At that point, I realized that my little girl had been using my toothbrush to scrub her personal toilet. Needless to say, I called in sick for the rest of the day.

I'm sure that you would agree, no matter what I did to that toothbrush, it would never be clean enough to be used again. Believe it or not, this story reveals an important spiritual truth. We've all been stained by sin. Despite our best efforts, we will never be clean enough or good enough for heaven. Forget about cleaning yourself up. Forget about breaking bad habits. None of that is good enough! There's only one way to become free from the contamination of sin. There's only one way to become clean in God's eyes.

The Bible says that if you confess your sins to Christ, He will forgive you and cleanse you from all unrighteousness. When you and I get honest with God and confess our sins to Christ, God promises to forgive us and cleanse us.

Here's the million-dollar question: If you know you sinned, and you know God saw you sin, and you know He promises to forgive whatever you confess, why not confess?

If you are reading this devotion and you haven't confessed your sins to Christ, then I encourage you to pray this prayer with me: "Lord Jesus, I confess that I have sinned. I ask You to forgive me of my sin. I ask You to cleanse me from the guilt of my sin. Become real and personal to me, Jesus. I surrender my life to You. Amen."

DOSE OF TRUTH

If we say that we have no sin, we deceive ourselves, and the truth is not in us. If we confess our sins, He is faithful and just to forgive us our sins and to cleanse us from all unrighteousness. **—1 John 1:8–9**

"Come now, and let us reason together," says the Lord, "Though your sins are like scarlet, they shall be as white as snow, though they are red like crimson, they shall be as wool." **—Isaiah 1:18**

It is a fearful thing to fall into the hands of the living God. **—Hebrews 10:31**

MAKIN' IT REAL

Have you ever met someone who said, "I'll go do the church thing once I break a few bad habits. Give me some time to get my life straight and then I'll give God a chance."

Why do people approach God this way?

What's wrong with this approach?

If we could clean ourselves up, why would we need a Savior?

How would you respond to someone who approaches God this way? Discuss your options with a friend.

DAY 5: **KEEP SWINGING**

A common mistake among many new Christians is to mess up, then give up. However, God never said that you could only receive forgiveness after the first confession. One boxer said, "I'm never down. I'm either up or I'm getting up." The Bible says that a righteous man falls seven times, but he will rise again. When you mess up, get up, 'fess up, and run toward God! Just because you fail, that doesn't mean you're a failure. Because of your relationship with Christ, you are more than a conqueror.

Think about Babe Ruth. Everyone associates his name with sports Hall of Fame, but did you know that he struck out over 1,330 times? There's one thing that separates average players from Hall of Famers—their passion to keep swinging. One pastor friend of mine says it this way: "I'm not asking you to be perfect. I'm simply asking you to never quit."

One old fella walked into an ice cream shop and saw a baseball team celebrating after their game. It seemed as though the attention revolved around one young boy at the head of the table. The man walked up and congratulated the team for their win.

The coach said, "Well thanks, but we didn't win."

The gentleman said, "Well, this one young man must have played a really good game."

The boy spoke up and said, "No sir, I struck out nine times today."

The confused man asked, "Well, why on earth are you celebrating?"

The coach said, "Because last week, he struck out ten times."

God *is* that coach. He is encouraging you to never give up. Just keep swinging!

Let me also add this bit of understanding . . . Grace is not only the forgiveness of sin, it's also the ability to stop sinning.

DOSE OF TRUTH

For a righteous man may fall seven times and rise again, but the wicked shall fall by calamity. —**Proverbs 24:16**

Who shall separate us from the love of Christ? Shall tribulation, or nakedness, or peril, or sword? As it is written: "For Your sake we are killed all day long; we are accounted as sheep for the slaughter." Yet in all these things we are more than conquerors through Him who loved us. For I am persuaded that neither death nor life, nor angels nor principalities nor powers, nor things present nor things to come, nor height nor depth, nor any other created thing, shall be able to separate us from the love of God which is in Christ Jesus our Lord.
—Romans 8:35–39

MAKIN' IT REAL

A sure sign of our level of spiritual maturity is how we respond when we sin and how we respond when someone else sins.

In today's story, how much do you have in common with the little boy at the head of the table, and how much do you have in common with the coach?

Make a point to encourage someone who has messed up lately.

Do you think some people take advantage of God's grace, using it as a crutch to continue sinning?

Do you actually think God can be taken advantage of?

What would you say to someone who pursues a lifestyle of sin while banking on grace?

DAY 6: **GETTIN' GOOD**

Many people make the assumption that we need to get good to get God. Actually, the opposite is true. We get God to get good. Let me explain it to you like this: if you're right on the inside, you'll do right on the outside.

One of Jesus' most passionate disciples was Peter. Peter had sworn publicly to support Christ no matter what. It wasn't long after that bold statement was made that Peter denied even knowing Jesus. The weight of Peter's sin became unbearable and under the load of guilt, Peter burst into tears. After the resurrection, Jesus found Peter and asked him, "Peter, do you love me?" Notice that Jesus didn't ask Peter why he did what he did. Notice that Jesus didn't ask Peter if he would ever do it again. Jesus simply asked, "Do you love me?" Christianity is about love not law, relationship not rules. It's a relationship that transforms us from the inside out. My obedience to the rules is a byproduct of my relationship with Jesus.

A hateful husband once demanded that his wife conform to a rigid set of standards of his own choosing. She was to do certain things for him as a wife, keep house a certain way, dress a certain way, treat the children a certain way, and speak and act in public a certain way. She tried to please her husband but over time, she came to hate his list of rules and regulations. Not surprisingly, she soon grew to hate him as well. Then, one day the man died—an act of God's mercy, as far as the wife was concerned.

Sometime later, she fell in love with another man and married him. To her surprise, she found that she and her new husband seemed to be on a perpetual honeymoon. Joyfully, she devoted herself to his good welfare. One day, while cleaning out some boxes in the attic, she came across one of the sheets of do's and don'ts her first husband had written for her to follow. To her amazement, she realized she was doing for her second husband all the things her first husband had demanded, even though her new husband had never once suggested them. Her behavior was no longer a chore, but a joyful expression of the love she had for her husband.

And so it must be with us and God. It's a relationship thing, not a rule thing! As you develop on the inside, you will see the results on the outside.

DOSE OF TRUTH

Then Jesus said to them, "All of you will be made to stumble because of Me this night, for it is written: 'I will strike the Shepherd, and the sheep of the flock will be scattered.' But after I have been raised, I will go before you to Galilee." Peter answered and said to Him, "Even if all are made to stumble because of You, I will never be made to stumble." Jesus said to him, "Assuredly, I say to you that this night, before the rooster crows, you will deny Me three times." Peter said to Him, "Even if I have to die with You, I will not deny You!" And so said all the disciples. **—Matthew 26:31–35**

This is now the third time Jesus showed Himself to His disciples after He was raised from the dead. So when they had eaten breakfast, Jesus said to Simon Peter, "Simon, son of Jonah, do you love Me . . .?" **—John 21:14–15**

MAKIN' IT REAL

How has your view of the Christian life changed over the last few days?

In your own opinion, what do most people think Christianity is all about?

If you had to define (for the whole world) in one sentence, what being a Christian is all about, what would your definition be?

DAY 7: **LOST SHEEP**

A few days after I became a Christian, I got myself into a compromising situation and I sinned, and I felt terrible. I wanted to talk to God about it, but I was too embarrassed. At that point, I had a choice to make. I could forget about the commitment I'd made to Christ and indulge in sin for the rest of my life, or I could confess what I had done and move forward.

Jesus once compared us to a sheep that wandered off from the flock. He asked, *"Which man of you, having a hundred sheep, if he loses one of them, does not leave the ninety-nine in the wilderness, and go after the one which is lost until he finds it? And when he has found it, he lays it on his shoulders, rejoicing."*

In the early days of my Christian journey, I lived under the fear of being rejected by God. I was so afraid of messing up. I pictured God with His arms folded in disbelief, waiting for me to screw something up.

But in the story of the lost sheep, Jesus gives us a much different picture of His thoughts toward us. In essence He says, "When you wander off, I will search for you until I find you. My love for you will never fade away. And when I find you, I won't say, 'I told you so.' I won't shame you or torment you. I'll pick you up. I'll put you on my shoulders like a father does his son, and I'll carry you home, rejoicing."

You never need to hide or run from God. Like I said earlier, one of Satan's biggest lies is that secret sins will remain hidden. Not so! Even the secret things belong to the Lord our God. May you never forget that He loves you more than you will ever know, and because of that love, you should always run *to* Him, never from Him.

DOSE OF TRUTH

Then all the tax collectors and the sinners drew near to Him to hear Him. And the Pharisees and scribes complained, saying, "This Man receives sinners and eats with them." So He spoke this parable to them, saying: "What man of you, having a hundred sheep, if he loses one of them, does not leave the ninety-nine in the wilderness, and go after the one which is lost until he finds it? And when he has found it, he lays it on his shoulders, rejoicing. And when he comes home, he calls together his friends and neighbors, saying to them, 'Rejoice with me, for I have found my sheep which was lost!' I say to you that likewise there will be some joy in heaven over one sinner who repents than over ninety-nine just persons who need no repentance." **—Luke 15:1–7**

The secret things belong to the Lord our God . . . **—Deuteronomy 29:29**

MAKIN' IT REAL

Have you ever felt like you were one goof-up away from being completely rejected by God?

If so, how does this belief affect your walk with the Lord?

How should you approach God when you stumble?

week 3
repentance / if none go with me

DAY 1: **U-TURN**

Look at salvation like a two-sided coin. On one side you have confession, and on the other side you have repentance. What's repentance? I'm glad you asked. Repentance means you go in the opposite direction. It's a change of course, a pursuit that leads you down a much different road.

There was a time in my life when I enjoyed the sin I was involved in, but after a while, what I once enjoyed left me feeling miserable. I was completely disgusted with sin. I wanted total freedom from my addictions. So, I confessed my sins to Christ, and I turned away from every compromising thing. For years, everything I indulged in fueled my hunger for ungodliness. The music I listened to, the movies I watched, and the concerts I attended all fed my craving for sin. Someone once said, "What goes in the well comes up in the pale." One night, I gathered up all my CD's, videos, magazines, and concert shirts, and I burned it all behind my house. As one of my friends used to say, "You can only love God as much as you hate sin."

The closer I got to God, the further I drifted from sin. My life was undergoing a huge transformation and I was loving every minute of it. I had discovered a freedom that was out of this world. I was intoxicated by the joy of the Lord.

The first message that Jesus ever preached was repentance. I'm convinced that everyone wants to go to heaven, but very few want to repent. Jesus said, "You can't have two masters. You'll love one and hate the other." His point was simple: you can't love God and love sin at the same time. A great Old Testament leader once said, "Make your choice today. Who are you going to serve? As for me and my house, we will serve the Lord."

DOSE OF TRUTH

Then Peter said to them, "Repent, and let every one of you be baptized in the name of Jesus Christ for the remission of sins . . ."
—Acts 2:38

For godly sorrow produces repentance leading to salvation . . .
—2 Corinthians 7:10

No servant can serve two masters; for either he will hate the one and love the other, or else he will be loyal to the one and despise the other . . . **—Luke 16:13**

"And if it seems evil to you to serve the Lord, chose for yourselves this day whom you will serve, whether the gods which your fathers served that were on the other side of the River, or the gods of the Amorites, in whose land you dwell. But as for me and my house, we will serve the Lord." **—Joshua 24:15**

MAKIN' IT REAL

Have you ever prayed, "God, if You will get me out of this mess, I promise I will never do this again"?

Did you do it again?

What's different about praying that prayer and truly repenting of your sin?

Many people have the attitude, "I'll sin now and confess later. If God forgave me once, He'll do it again." Is that an attitude of repentance? Take a few minutes and explain your answer.

DAY 2: **POTHOLES**

A friend of mine once said that there's a big difference between falling into temptation and walking into temptation. He said, "Falling into temptation is when I'm blindsided by temptation. Walking into temptation is when I willfully place myself in a compromising situation that tempts me at my point of weakness."

One of my favorite stories is called *An Autobiography in Five Short Chapters*. Trust me; nothing illustrates avoiding temptation quite like this. Check it out:

CHAPTER 1
I walk down the street. There's a deep hole in the sidewalk. I fall in. I'm helpless. It isn't my fault. It takes a long time to find a way out.

CHAPTER 2
I walk down the same street. There's a deep hole in the sidewalk. I pretend I don't see it. I fall in again. I can't believe I'm in the same place, but it isn't my fault. It still takes a long time to get out.

CHAPTER 3
I walk down the same street. There's a deep hole in the sidewalk. I see it's there. I still fall in. Now it's a habit. My eyes are opened. I know where I am. I confess it's my fault. I get out immediately.

CHAPTER 4
I walk down the same street. There's a deep hole in the sidewalk. I walk around it.

CHAPTER 5
I walk down a different street. Get the point?

In **1 Corinthians**, the Bible says that no temptation has come your way that is not common to all mankind, but God is faithful. He will not let you be tempted beyond what you can bear; He will show you how to escape temptation's power. Not only is God able to save you, He is also able to keep you. In the face of every temptation, God promises to provide you with a way to escape.

DOSE OF TRUTH

If I say, "My foot slips," Your mercy, O Lord, will hold me up. **—Psalm 94:18**

You have also given me the shield of Your salvation; Your right hand has held me up, Your gentleness has made me great. You enlarge my path under me, so my feet did not slip. **—Psalm 18:35–36**

No temptation has overtaken you except such as is common to man; but God is faithful, who will not allow you to be tempted beyond what you are able, but with the temptation will also make the way of escape, that you may be able to bear it. **—1 Corinthians 10:13**

MAKIN' IT REAL

Is it a sin to be tempted?

When does temptation give way to sin?

Do you regularly allow yourself to get into compromising situations that tempt you at your point of weakness? Yes? Never? Sometimes?

If you answered yes or sometimes, then what are you going to do differently?

DAY 3: **AVOIDING TEMPTATION**

Begin now to intentionally avoid temptation. You're probably thinking, *How in the world can someone avoid temptation?* I know we can't avoid all temptation, but many times, we sabotage our walk with God by flirting with our weaknesses. Read the verse below:

"But each one is tempted when he is drawn away by his own desire and enticed" (**James 1:14**).

This verse raises two very important questions:

1. What am I tempted by the most? This is the enticing desire that James refers to.
2. When am I tempted the most? This is the drawing away that James refers to.

By answering those two questions, you can avoid a lot of trouble. For example, if you struggle with Internet porn and you have a computer in your bedroom, or a private study area, move it to the living room! The first time your momma catches you getting an eye full, she will personally see to it that God sets you free. This may sound simple, but a little common sense will go a long way.

There's an old story about a wise Cherokee chief and his grandson. As the chief was nearing death, he told his grandson, "There are two wolves inside every man. One is evil and seeks to destroy. The other wolf is good and full of peace, joy, life, and seeks the best for all men. These two wolves war against one another, seeking to dominate our thoughts and choices." The grandson asked, "Which wolf wins?" The wise chief said, "The one you feed."

Romans 8:1 says, "There is therefore now no condemnation (no damnation or eternal punishment of sin) to those who are in Christ Jesus, who do not walk according to the flesh, but according to the Spirit." Notice the word Spirit is capitalized. This is a reference to the Holy Spirit or the Spirit of God. So what would it mean to walk according to the Spirit? On the flipside, what do you think it means to walk according to the flesh?

DOSE OF TRUTH

Blessed *is* the man who endures temptation; for when he has been approved, he will receive the crown of life which the Lord has promised to those who love Him. Let no one say when he is tempted, "I am tempted by God"; for God cannot be tempted by evil, nor does He Himself tempt anyone. But each one is tempted when he is drawn away by his own desires and enticed. Then, when desire has conceived, it gives birth to sin; and sin, when it is full-grown, brings forth death. **—James 1:12–15**

MAKIN' IT REAL

You may need an additional sheet of paper for these two questions:

What sin or sins do you struggle with the most?

When do you find yourself struggling the most?

Now, spend time brainstorming solutions to avoiding those situations. Make a plan and stick to it.

DAY 4: **PLAN OF ACTION**

In the book of Genesis, we find the story of Joseph. In Chapter 39, Joseph is managing the estate of Potiphar, a high-ranking officer in Egypt. Potiphar's wife was attracted to Joseph, and she made her affection known to Joseph day after day. However, Joseph loved God, and every time she came on to him, he turned her down. Then, one day, Joseph went to work at Potiphar's house. Little did he know, Potiphar's wife was home alone. She grabbed his shirt and demanded that he take her to bed. The Bible said that Joseph jerked away from her so hard that his shirt was ripped off his back and, without hesitating, he ran outside.

Many times, we get ourselves into trouble because we haven't posted boundaries around our areas of weakness. Trust me; it's easier to stand against the pressure of temptation when you've thought through your convictions long before the temptation comes your way. Long before Joseph found himself alone with Potiphar's wife, he developed a plan of action. When faced with the temptation, he knew what to do.

Consider what Joseph did not do:

He did not ignore the woman.
He did not try to lead the woman in prayer.
He did not try to reason with the woman.
He did not try to share his faith with the woman.

So what did he do?

He jerked away.
He ran outside.
He surrounded himself with other people.
He overcame the temptation.
He won the battle.

DOSE OF TRUTH

He who walks with wise men will be wise, but the companion of fools will be destroyed. **—Proverbs 13:20**

Blessed is the man who walks not in the counsel of the ungodly . . . **—Psalm 1:1**

Be sober, be vigilant, because your adversary the devil walks about like a roaring lion, seeking whom he may devour. **—1 Peter 5:8**

MAKIN' IT REAL

Many times, it's not just a situation that tempts us. Most of the time it's a certain person or a group of people we run with who really light our temptation fuse. How should you approach these folks the next time they call on you?

How do you take a strong stand for what you believe in without being a spiritual jerk?

DAY 5: **IFFY THINGS**

"Therefore, we also, since we are surrounded by so great a cloud of witnesses, let us lay aside every weight, and the sin which so easily ensnares us, and let us run with endurance the race that is set before us" (**Hebrews 12:1**).

For years, that verse has left me scratching my head. God encourages us to lay aside every weight, and the sin, which so easily ensnares us. Now, I know what sin is, but what's a weight? Remember, the book of Hebrews was originally written in Greek. The Greek word that was translated as weight actually means "a swelling tumor." I call these weights iffy things.

Iffy things are those areas in our lives that aren't clearly defined in the Bible as sin. They're those things that cause us to ask, "Is this okay? I really don't know *if* this is a sin or not, so I'll just keep doing it until God tells me otherwise." The Bible not only tells us to flee from evil, but also the appearance of evil. Iffy things hinder your relationship with Christ in two ways:

1. Iffy things keep you from approaching the throne of God with boldness. When you're tangled up in iffy things, all you can think about when you pray is, "Lord, is this stuff sin or not?"
2. Iffy things rob you of the confidence you need. Someone once said, "You can't stand against the devil if you're unsure how you stand with God." How true that is!

What keeps most Christians from being world changers is not outright sin. It's not lying, stealing, getting drunk, and smoking pot. It's the iffy things that keep us from being what God has called us to be. It's giving God 95 percent of our lives, and then filling the other 5 percent with iffy things, that makes us weak people.

DOSE OF TRUTH

Flee also youthful lusts; but pursue righteousness, faith, love, peace with those who call on the Lord out of a pure heart. **—2 Timothy 2:22**

Test all things; hold fast what is good. Abstain from every form of evil. **—1 Thessalonians 5:21–22**

. . . the Lord knows how to deliver the godly out of temptations and to reserve the unjust under punishment for the day of judgment. **—2 Peter 2:9**

For in that He Himself has suffered, being tempted, He is able to aid those who are tempted. **—Hebrews 2:18**

MAKIN' IT REAL

Are you tangled in iffy things? If so, believe me, having a stronger will power just won't cut it. Freedom is found in our relationship with Christ. Set some God-time goals. Start praying and study the Bible with a Christian friend. Hold each other accountable. The closer you get to the fire of God's presence, the more life's trash is burned away.

Do you think that God ever expected us to be able to live right by our own will power? Don't limit your answer to a simple yes or no. Talk it through.

Take a few minutes to set some God-time goals.

DAY 6: **CHAINED UP**

A preacher once told a story about two guys who were restoring an old car. Their project was one small part away from completion. A nearby farmer had several broken-down vintage automobiles piled on one end of his pasture. The two guys decided to pay the farmer a visit. The farmer said, "I'm sure I've got the part you're looking for. Just look around and take whatever you need, but be on the lookout for my dog, boys. It will attack!"

As they walked through the junked cars, they came upon a huge hole in the ground. One fella picked up a rock and threw it in the hole. He leaned over to hear the rock hit bottom, but heard nothing. He picked up an old battery and threw it in, and still heard nothing. At that point, the other fella picked up a heavy steel wheel and threw it in the hole. About that time, the old man's dog came running out from behind a car, barking and foaming at the mouth. The dog ran right by both men and jumped straight down the dark hole.

The farmer came running across the field and asking, "What happened? I heard my dog barking. Are you guys all right?" One of the men spoke up and said, "Sir, we're okay, but that dog of yours jumped down in this big hole." The farmer said, "That's impossible! I had that dog chained to a heavy steel wheel."

Even after we become Christians, we can get chained to the wrong things. The ironic thing about sin is that it almost always begins with positive benefits. You do something wrong and lie about it; you avoid the punishment. You have sex outside of marriage and you experience the pleasures of sin. However, at some point, what begins as pleasure, becomes a prison.

Over the past fifteen years, I've visited many incarcerated young people. In every situation, their story began with a bunch of friends having fun, acting crazy. One by one I've heard them all say, "Me and my friends this," and "Me and my friends that." In the beginning, they were surrounded by peers, but the end was total isolation. I'll never forget John. He told me fifty to sixty people would party at his house every weekend. John had been in prison for over six years.

Since the day he was arrested, not one person had come to visit. It's true that there's pleasure in sin, but it's only for a season.

DOSE OF TRUTH

Jesus answered them, "Most assuredly, I say to you, whoever commits sin is a slave of sin." **—John 8:34**

"Therefore if the Son makes you free, you shall be free indeed." **—John 8:36**

Stand fast therefore in the liberty by which Christ has made us free, and do not be entangled again with a yoke of bondage. **—Galatians 5:1**

MAKIN' IT REAL

Do you know anyone imprisoned by sin?

What are some action steps you can take to help this person find freedom?

DAY 7: **JUSTIFIABLE INSANITY**

I'm one of those people who shuffles around the junk on their desk, but never quite finds a place for most of it. I only organize the clutter when I misplace something important. For two weeks, I've noticed a CD lying on top of my computer tower. The word "desperation" is printed across the face of the disc. I've used that word many times, but what does it really mean? Webster's Dictionary defines desperation as "intense situations that involve extreme danger or possible disaster." For two weeks, this word has possessed my thoughts. I believe desperation can be defined with two words: justifiable insanity.

If I told you that a man cut off his own arm and drank his own urine for several days, you would say, "He's insane! Lock him up and throw away the key!" But Aron Ralston did just that, and he wasn't crazy; he was desperate.

On April 26, 2003, Ralston, a rock climber, got himself into trouble. He had taken a few days off work and told no one where he was going. During a hike in a canyon in Utah, he was passing through a risky spot between two rocky cliffs when a giant rock fell from the top of the cliff ledge and landed on his arm, pinning him to the cliff side. Day after day a raven would circle the sky above Ralston, eagerly anticipating its next meal. When his water ran out, he was forced to drink his own urine to keep from dying of dehydration. After several days, Aron had no other alternative. He took out his pocket knife and cut off his own arm.

There's a fine line between desperation and insanity, and 99.9 percent of the time, the only thing that separates one from the other is a justifiable situation—a situation that calls for insane actions—but because the situation demands it, we call it desperation.

Are you desperate in your pursuit of Jesus? If so, God gives you a wonderful promise. **Jeremiah 33:3** says, "Call on Me, and I'll answer you, and I'll show you great and mighty things that you know not of."

Someone once told me, "You are as close to God as you want to be." To be honest, the statement offended me. I thought, *No I'm not! I long to be closer, nearer, more intimate, to be wrapped up in Him.*

Before I could say anything in disagreement, **James 4:8** rose up in me: "Draw near to God and He will draw near to you." His statement was true. Desperation creates motivation. If you're desperate for something, you will do anything to get more of it.

DOSE OF TRUTH

Blessed are those who hunger and thirst for righteousness, for they shall be filled. **—Matthew 5:6**

. . . Jesus stood and cried out, saying, "If anyone thirsts, let him come to Me and drink." **—John 7:37**

MAKIN' IT REAL

Have you ever been truly desperate for something? What was it?

What is the most extreme measure you've ever taken to get something?

Do you want to be crazy-in-love with God? Then make this prayer a part of your daily routine:

Lord, forgive me for being desperate for so many things other than You. Thank You for the passionate love You have for me. Make me hungry for You. Cause my hunger for You to outgrow my hunger for anything else. Your Word says that if I ask, I shall receive, so today I ask for holy desperation. Amen.

week 4
connection / preparing for opposition

DAY 1: **GETTING CONNECTED**

For years, I wanted to have a genuine relationship with God. However, I was so entangled in my sinful addictions that I eventually abandoned all hope of being free. I assumed the only people who could live for Christ were the social outcasts. These were the people who were never invited to the parties I frequently attended. I truly believed that I could never be free from the guilt and shame that my addictions brought me.

One Sunday morning, I went to church with my mom. In a desperate attempt to find peace with God, I went forward. When the service was over, I walked straight up to the edge of the stage and whispered to the person closest to me, "I need help. I want to be saved, but I need help." From that moment on, my life began to radically change. Yes, I confessed my sin to Christ, but I also made myself accountable to another believer.

I started meeting with the church's youth pastor on a regular basis. He was twice my age and had a great reputation as a seasoned youth minister. I held nothing back. After revealing to him my struggles, I remember saying, "The next time you see me, ask me how I'm doing." That accountability relationship changed my life.

Show me who your friends are, and I'll show you who you are soon to be. Ask yourself, "Who am I connected to? Who is helping me more deeply develop my walk with God?"

DOSE OF TRUTH

And the Lord God said, "It is not good that man should be alone . . ." **—Genesis 2:18**

Though one may be overpowered by another, two can withstand him. And a threefold cord is not quickly broken. **—Ecclesiastes 4:12**

"For where two or three are gathered together in My name, I am there in the midst of them." **—Matthew 18:20**

Do not love the world or the things in the world. If anyone loves the world, the love of the Father is not in him. For all that is in the world—the lust of the flesh, the lust of the eyes, and the pride of life—is not of the Father but is of the world. And the world is passing away, and the lust of it; but he who does the will of God abides forever. **—1 John 2:15–17**

MAKIN' IT REAL

Have you ever bought into the lie that you will never be able to live an authentic Christian life?

Do you currently have an accountability partner: someone who encourages you to more earnestly pursue God? If you answered no, ask God to direct you to the right person.

Take a few minutes and begin making a list of people you know who could possibly play that role in your life.

DAY 2: **ACCOUNTABILITY TIPS**

Accountability is a must-have for every Christian. **Proverbs 27:17** says, "As iron sharpens iron, so one man sharpens another."

I remember the first time I saw Sylvester Stallone play Rocky Balboa. I went home and beat on everything in sight. I curled rocks in my backyard to pump my biceps. I used a tree limb for a chin-up bar. I even used my little brother as a punching bag. You see, when you witness someone excel at something, you become motivated to reach for a higher level of excellence. Why? Because passion is contagious! If you want to make an impact on your world for Christ, get around someone who's already impacting his or hers.

James 5:16 says, "Confess your trespasses to one another, and pray for one another, that you may be healed. The effective, fervent prayer of a righteous man avails much." Notice there's a direct connection between godly accountability and deliverance or healing.

As important as accountability is, you don't want to link arms with just anybody. Let me give you some accountability tips:

- You need to be accountable to someone who's more mature in their faith than you.
- Your accountability partner should be of the same gender as you.
- This person should have a great reputation among the leaders in your church.
- Connect with someone you can trust to keep your discussions confidential. Remember, the reason a dog has so many friends is because he wags his tail and not his tongue.
- Your accountability partner should be someone you enjoy being with. There's an old saying that goes, "A real friend is someone who puts a finger on your faults without rubbing them in."

DOSE OF TRUTH

Two are better than one, because they have a good reward for their labor. For if they fall, one will lift up his companion. But woe to him who is alone when he falls, for he has no one to help him up. **—Ecclesiastes 4:9-10**

Remember your leaders, who spoke the word of God to you. Consider the outcome of their way of life and imitate their faith. **—Hebrews 13:7 (New International Version)**

MAKIN' IT REAL

Who did you want to be like when you were a kid and why?

Why does being around achieving people create a desire in you to achieve?

Who are your spiritual heroes?

DAY 3: THE WRONG CROWD

In **2 Samuel 13**, the Bible tells the story of a young man by the name of Amnon. Amnon had a beautiful half sister named Tamar. The Bible says that Amnon loved his sister Tamar, but this was not your typical brother-sister love. Amnon struggled with lustful thoughts toward his sister, and eventually he raped her. Now believe it or not, I think Amnon was a pretty good kid, and let me explain why. As the story begins, Amnon is fighting the war against lust. He becomes so vexed by his thoughts that he soon develops an ulcer. Amnon literally got sick at the thought of sin. We all know people who don't give sin a second thought, they just do it, but Amnon was not that kind of guy. The thought of sin made him physically ill.

Five words, found in verse three, reveal Amnon's greatest problem:

"But Amnon had a friend . . ."

The friend's name was Jonadab. Jonadab encouraged Amnon's sinful appetite. It was Jonadab who gave Amnon the plan to follow through and rape Tamar.

This story takes a more interesting twist when you look closely at the names of these two young men. Amnon's name means "a faithful brother." Jonadab's name means "God is liberal." Now think about this for moment. One godly young man listened to an ungodly friend, and the destiny of his life was destroyed.

When Amnon's brother found out what he had done to their sister, he had Amnon murdered. **Proverbs 12:26** says, "The righteous should choose his friends carefully, for the way of the wicked leads them astray."

DOSE OF TRUTH

The righteous should choose his friends carefully, for the way of the wicked leads them astray. **—Proverbs 12:26**

"And I say to you, My friends, do not be afraid of those who kill the body, and after that have no more that they can do. But I will show you whom you should fear: Fear Him who, after He has killed, has power to cast into hell; yes, I say to you, fear Him! Are not five sparrows sold for two copper coins? And not one of them is forgotten before God. But the very hairs of your head are all numbered. Do not fear therefore; you are of more value than many sparrows." **—Luke 12:4–7**

For we have spent enough of our past lifetime in doing the will of the Gentiles—when we walked in lewdness, lusts, drunkenness, revelries, drinking parties, and abominable idolatries. In regard to these, they think it strange that you do not run with them in the same flood of dissipation, speaking evil of you. **—1 Peter 4:3–4**

MAKIN' IT REAL

Has anyone ever gotten you into major trouble? What happened?

Do you believe that your friends really affect the kind of person you are?

1 Corinthians 15:33 says, "Do not be deceived: 'Evil company corrupts good habits.'" If your friends are a reflection of who you are soon to be, then who are you becoming?

DAY 4: **BEING SWAYED**

Here's the big question: should a Christian befriend a non-Christian? I've heard both extremes. One person says, "Jesus befriended sinful people, so we should too." Someone else will say, "The Bible says, 'Don't be unequally yoked together with unbelievers.'" So what do we do?

The Bible does not contradict itself on this issue. Yes, Jesus did befriend sinful people, but He only became closely connected to those people He could sway. Those He could not sway, He let go on their way. In **Matthew 19**, Jesus challenged one young man to sell all he had and become His disciple. The young man turned down the offer, and Jesus watched him walk away.

Jesus never negotiated with anyone. He made His business very clear. He was on a mission, and everyone around Him knew it. The mission of Christ was to please His Heavenly Father. As Christians, that's our mission too.

So, to answer the big question, yes, we should be friends with non-Christian people. Our mission is winning others to Christ. However, in every relationship, we need to ask ourselves a few important questions:

- Who's being swayed here?
- Am I swaying this person to Christ, or is this person swaying me away from Christ?"
- Do my friends know that I'm on a mission to please God?

DOSE OF TRUTH

Do not be unequally yoked together with unbelievers. For what fellowship has righteousness with lawlessness? And what communion has light with darkness? **—2 Corinthians 6:14**

". . . come out from among them and be separate," says the Lord. "Do not touch what is unclean, and I will receive you." **—2 Corinthians 6:17**

Adulterers and adulteresses! Do you not know that friendship with the world is enmity with God? Whoever therefore wants to be a friend of the world makes himself an enemy of God. **—James 4:4**

MAKIN' IT REAL

Make a list of all your closest friends and then ask yourself, "Who's being swayed? Am I swaying them, or are they swaying me?"

Friendship Quiz

Friend's name	They're being swayed	I'm being swayed
_____	_____	_____
_____	_____	_____
_____	_____	_____
_____	_____	_____
_____	_____	_____
_____	_____	_____

DAY 5: **THREE'S NOT A CROWD**

Every follower of Christ needs the following three relationships:

1. Someone you're reaching up to
2. Someone you're reaching down to
3. Someone walking beside you

Several years ago, William and Howard Hendricks wrote a book titled *As Iron Sharpens Iron*. The authors make this incredible statement: "Refuse to believe the lie of the devil that says only weak men need help. The truth is, it is men who seek help who become strong."[4]

Regardless of where we are in our relationship with Christ, we should all be reaching up to someone who is further up the spiritual ladder than we are. I could never express to you in words how important this is! It's equally important that you reach down to someone who is not at your level of spiritual maturity.

Think of the Christian life as a chain of people linked together, being pulled by the Holy Spirit closer to the heart of God. Each link is passionately loved by God. Ask yourself, "How long is my spiritual chain? How many lives is my life affecting?"

Last, but not least, we all need someone climbing beside us. Everyone needs a friend they can grow with, learn with, and achieve with. The ministry of Jesus contained these three relationships. When He sent out His twelve disciples, He sent them out in groups of two. Every disciple had someone beside them. Every disciple was sent to reach down to those who had fallen away from God. Every disciple had Jesus to reach up to. Does your life contain these three relationships?

DOSE OF TRUTH

"These things I command you, that you love one another." **—John 15:17**

new.u

Let no one despise your youth, but be an example to the believers in word, in conduct, in love, in spirit, in faith, in purity. **—1 Timothy 4:12**
And let us consider one another in order to stir up love and good works, not forsaking the assembling of ourselves together, as is the manner of some, but exhorting one another, and so much the more as you see the day approaching. **—Hebrews 10:24–25**

MAKIN' IT REAL

Have you ever shared one of your struggles with someone? If so, how did it feel after you unloaded the truth?

How long is your spiritual chain? How many people are you reaching up to, out to, and down to?

DAY 6: **SUPERNATURAL POWER**

As a follower of Christ, you now have incredible support from heaven. God has hooked you up in two major ways:

1. He has given you His Spirit
2. He has given you His angels for protection

In **Acts 1:8**, Jesus said, "You will receive power after the Holy Spirit has come upon you." Many years ago, a fella by the name of Albert Noble was experimenting with nitroglycerin. He soon invented an explosive device that would revolutionize the way we mined for minerals and fought battles. Naming his invention was perhaps the most difficult task of all. Then, one day he came across the Greek word used in **Acts 1:8**. The Greek word used for power is *dunamis*, which means "incredible, supernatural power." Albert Noble named his explosive "dynamite" after the Greek word *dunamis*.

See, God has given His children power. God knew that in our greatest efforts we couldn't live the Christian life. There's only been one man who could live a sinless life, and that man was Jesus Christ. So, the One who could live it came to die for the ones who could not live it. When Jesus rose from the dead, He sent His Spirit to empower us. So now, the Spirit of the One who *could* live it lives in those who *can't* live it. This means that the ones who could not live it now have the power to live it.

Before you came to Christ, the Spirit of God worked endlessly to bring you to Christ. Now that you're following Christ, the Spirit of God works endlessly to keep you and empower you to live like Christ. Before Jesus was crucified, He told His disciples that He would not leave them as orphans, but promised to send to them the Holy Spirit. The Bible says that we are the temple of the Holy Spirit. Think about it! If you follow Christ, the God who formed the universe now lives and dwells inside of you. Begin to thank the Lord for giving you His Spirit, and daily ask Him to fill your life with power.

Psalms 91:11 says that God has given His angels charge over you to keep you in all your ways. I grew up thinking that everyone had their own guardian angel. However, the Bible says that each child of God is surrounded by the angels of heaven. Now think about this. In **2 Kings 18** and **19**, the Bible says that God's people were being oppressed by the Assyrian army. King Hezekiah ruled over Israel during this time and he began crying out to God for help. The Bible says that one night an angel came down while the Assyrian army slept, and that one angel killed 185,000 Assyrian soldiers. Now, if one angel killed 185,000 armed soldiers, and we are surrounded by angels, why would we ever bow to anything but God?

DOSE OF TRUTH

For He shall give His angels charge over you, to keep you in all your ways, in their hands they shall bear you up, lest you dash your foot against a stone. You shall tread upon the lion and the cobra, the young lion and the serpent you shall trample underfoot. **—Psalm 91:11–13**

The angel of the Lord encamps all around those who fear Him, and delivers them. **—Psalm 34:7**

You are of God, little children, and have overcome them, because He who is in you is greater than he who is in the world. **—1 John 4:4**

MAKIN' IT REAL

Did you grow up believing that you had your own personal guardian angel? If so, describe the way you envisioned that angel. What was your mental picture of that angel? Did he abandon ship if you broke the speed limit?

How has today's devotion changed the way you view the Holy Spirit and angels?

How has today's devotion affected the way you view yourself as a child of God?

DAY 7: **GO**

During my senior year of high school, my dad bought me a sweet convertible IROC Z28. The day I got it, I put one hundred miles on it just cruising around our small town. I was excited about my new car and I wanted to share my excitement with others.

During that same year, I was given another gift, one far greater than my new Z28. I was given the gift of eternal life. You better believe I wanted everyone to know it! You don't have to know a thousand Bible verses to share with someone what Jesus has done in your life. See, the Bible is very clear—everyone will spend eternity somewhere. Heaven's real and so is hell. These are the choices we have to choose from. As Christians, we have a great responsibility placed upon our shoulders. I heard one minister say, "Two-thirds of God's name spells the word 'Go.'" God has commanded us to go.

Now, God hasn't gifted me with a lot of boldness. Put me in a crowded room full of strangers and I'll be the guy sitting in the corner reading a good book. But think about this for a second: if you saw someone blindly walking into a pit of fire, no matter what your personality type is, you would quickly and boldly respond. Now, I don't suggest that you preach hellfire and brimstone to everyone you run into—be creative but also be active.

When I go out to eat and the waiter brings me my food, I often say, "Hey, I'm about to pray over my food; do you have a prayer request? I'd love to pray for ya." It's amazing how that simple nonthreatening question opens the door for ministry. I once sat in a five-star restaurant and had a waitress tear up and pour her heart out to me and a couple of friends. Her dad was a minister who had recently passed away and she hadn't attended a church service in several years. God was tugging at her heart and she just broke. If we'll be bold and let God use us, we'll be amazed at how many lives He can touch through us.

DOSE OF TRUTH

You are the light of the world. A city that is set on a hill cannot be hidden. Nor do they light a lamp and put it under a basket, but on a lampstand, and it gives light to all who are in the house. Let your light so shine before men, that they may see your good works and glorify your Father in heaven. **—Matthew 5:14–16**

MAKIN' IT REAL

List some creative ways that you can share your faith with the people around you.

Here are some helpful tips on sharing your story:

1. What was your life like before you came to know Christ?

2. Describe how you became a Christian. What happened? Where were you?

3. How has your life changed now that you know Christ?

week 5
devotion / a different purpose

DAY 1: **BRAINWASHED**

The first six months of my journey with Jesus were the most difficult days of my life. For many years, I had filled my mind with every form of ungodliness. I assumed that once I confessed my sin, God would erase all the impure thoughts from my memory bank. When that didn't happen, I questioned whether I was really saved at all. I felt clean and pure inside, but my mind was consumed with filthy thoughts. Then someone shared these verses with me:

Romans 12:1–2 says, "I beseech you therefore, brethren, that ye present your bodies a living sacrifice, holy, acceptable unto God which is your reasonable service. And be not conformed to this world but be ye transformed by the renewing of your mind . . ."

Notice here that the key to transformation is the renewing of your mind. If you are a new Christian, don't beat yourself up if you struggle with memories and pictures of ungodliness. Please understand that renewing your mind takes time! The more you fill your mind with God's Word, the less your mind will be filled with ungodly thoughts. If you pump your mind full of garbage, don't expect to think about anything other than garbage. Here are some practical tips on renewing your mind:

- Study God's Word
- Listen to the Bible on CD—on your way to school, as you mow the lawn, as you sleep at night. I did this faithfully throughout my first year as a Christian.
- Study God's Word with a small group of your friends.
- Memorize verses that assure your victory.

DOSE OF TRUTH

I will meditate on Your precepts, and contemplate Your ways. I will delight myself in Your statutes; I will not forget Your word. **—Psalm 119:15–16**

Then Jesus said to those Jews who believed Him, "If you abide in My word, you are My disciples indeed. And you shall know the truth, and the truth shall make you free." **—John 8:31–32**

Let this mind be in you which was also in Christ Jesus. **—Philippians 2:5**

Be anxious for nothing, but in everything by prayer and supplication, with thanksgiving, let your request by made known to God; and the peace of God, which surpasses all understanding, will guard your hearts and minds through Christ Jesus. Finally, brethren, whatever things are true, whatever things are noble, whatever things are just, whatever things are pure, whatever things are lovely, whatever things are of a good report, if there is any virtue and if there is anything praiseworthy—meditate on these things. **—Philippians 4:6–8**

MAKIN' IT REAL

Why doesn't God simply erase our minds of impure thoughts when we give our hearts to Him?

All of us have bad thoughts race through our minds from time to time, but are these thoughts sin? If not, when do they become sin?

Read Psalm 119:15–16. Have you ever been so obsessed by something that you just couldn't get it off your mind? Maybe it was an upcoming vacation or a new pair of shoes. What was it? Ask the Lord to give you that same obsession for His Word.

DAY 2: **TRUTH: CONFIDENCE CLEANSING**

By the time you graduate high school, you will have received 11,000 hours of instruction. That's a whole lot of information. Now ask yourself, "How much biblical instruction have I received during these years?" Would you say that you know more about arithmetic than you know about God's Word?

Please don't misunderstand me—a great education is extremely important. However, I guarantee you, when you arrive at the pearly gates, Peter will not hand you a calculus test.

Let me share with you three reasons why the Bible is so important:

1. It is our source of absolute truth
2. It is our source of healthy confidence
3. It is our source of daily cleansing

Absolute Truth

Pretend that you and I had an argument over how many inches are in a foot. How would we determine who was right and who was wrong? Absolutes may not be politically correct in our society today, but like it or not, there is a right and wrong answer here. To find the answer, we must go to the standard. The headquarters of the International Bureau of Weights and Measurements is located in a suburb of Paris. This organization sets the standard for all weights and measurements. Their standard transcends anyone's opinion and points us all in the right direction.

Just as there's a standard for weights and measurements, there's also a standard for right and wrong. That standard is the Holy Bible. The Word of God is concrete and unshakable—it will not change.

Healthy Confidence

The reason most people yield to peer pressure is because they lack confidence. Confidence gives you the ability to stand up when everyone else bows down. The only way to obtain a healthy dose of confidence is to see yourself through the eyes of a loving God who created you with unique abilities and talents.

Daily Cleansing

The Word of God is an incredible source of daily cleansing. In **Psalm 119:11**, King David said to God, "Your word I have hidden in my heart, that I might not sin against You." Jesus said to His disciples, "Now you are clean through the word which I have spoken to you."

DOSE OF TRUTH

I have restrained my feet from every evil way, that I may keep Your word. I have not departed from Your judgments, for You Yourself have taught me. How sweet are Your words to my taste, sweeter than honey to my mouth! Through Your precepts I get understanding; therefore I hate every false way. Your word is a lamp to my feet and a light to my path. **—Psalm 119:101–105**

. . . I have written to you, young men, because you are strong, and the word of God abides in you, and you have overcome the wicked one. **—1 John 2:14**

MAKIN' IT REAL

Most people make ungodly decisions due to a lack of confidence. Confidence enables you to stand up and be different. On a scale from 1–10 where's your confidence level?

Are you cleansing yourself daily with God's Word?

DAY 3: **THIRTY-DAY CHALLENGE**

Studies reveal that anything we do for thirty days becomes a habit. For the next thirty days, I want to challenge you to set a time each day to read God's Word and pray. The book of John is the fourth book of the New Testament, and it's a great place to start reading.

Now, reading is something we all understand, but prayer can be a confusing concept for some people. Prayer is simply our conversation time with God. It's a time when God and I embrace one another in an intimate relationship, and the power of His Spirit is increased in my life. Someone once told me that seven days without prayer makes one *weak*—not week, but weak.

My personal prayer time is early in the morning. I get away from anything that might distract me from focusing on Christ. I turn the lights down low, and put on my favorite Christian worship CD. I sing to the Lord. I thank Him for all He's done in my life. I confess to Him my struggles. I ask for more of His thoughts, passions, and desires to be my thoughts, passions, and desires. I daily ask Him to burn out everything in me that's not like Him. You get the picture!

When you pray, I encourage you to do two things:

1. Get a prayer partner—someone marked by God. Listen to them pray. Learn from their prayer time. Ask questions.
2. Pray the Word of God. I have a list of verses that I often refer to when I pray. If I need wisdom for a decision, I remind God of **James 1:5**: "If any man lacks wisdom, let him ask of God, who gives to all liberally and without reproach, and it will be given to him."

You'll be amazed at how a few minutes with God will affect your life. In **Genesis chapter 32**, Jacob had an encounter with God and went from being called Jacob, which means "deceiver," to being called Israel, which means "a prince with God." In **Judges 6**, Gideon had an encounter with God and went from wimp to warrior! In **Isaiah 6:1-8**, Isaiah saw the Lord and he went from an unclean man to an on-fire prophet! Encountering God daily in prayer will change your life!

DOSE OF TRUTH

I cried to the Lord with my voice and He heard me from His holy hill. **—Psalm 3:4**

. . . the Lord will hear when I call to Him. **—Psalm 4:3**

Now this is the confidence that we have in Him, that if we ask anything according to His will, He hears us. And if we know that He hears us, whatever we ask, we know that we have the petitions that we have asked of Him. **—1 John 5:14–15**

MAKIN' IT REAL

Do you spend more time talking on the phone than you do talking to God? If you're like most people, the answer is a big fat YES! When you have a problem, why is it easier to talk to a friend than it is to God?

I've listed some awesome Scripture references concerning God encounters. Take some time today to read through these passages:

Exodus 19:16–19
Isaiah 6:1–8
Daniel 10:10–12
Acts 9:1–6
Revelation 1:9–17

DAY 4: THE WAR

Buckle your seatbelt: today I want to talk to you about spiritual warfare. I'm not trying to freak you out or anything, but the Bible makes it very clear that there's a spiritual war going on right now. I know it sounds like a sci-fi flick, but it's clearly revealed throughout God's Word from cover to cover. In **2 Timothy 6:12**, the Bible calls the Christian journey, "the good fight of faith." You can't have a fight without an opponent. Scripture says that Satan roams around like a roaring lion seeking whom he may devour.

Before I became a Christian, the choices I made were influenced by hell. After I became a follower of Christ, a major conflict began. There were certain sinful habits that I was instantly set free from, but other addictions pulled at me. In Judges, chapters two and three, the Bible says that God allowed wicked nations to dwell in the land that He had given to His people. He did this so that future generations would learn how to wage war. God wants you to learn how to fight against the sinful temptations of this world.

If you're going to be an effective soldier, you must give yourself to the Word of God and prayer. In his book, *The Three Battlegrounds*, Francis Frangipane writes: "You will remember that the location where Jesus was crucified was called 'Golgotha,' which meant 'place of the skull.' If we will be effective in spiritual warfare, the first field of conflict where we must learn warfare is the battleground of the mind; the 'place of the skull.' To defeat the devil, we must be renewed in our minds."[5]

Ephesians 6 lists the spiritual armor of the Christian soldier. What's so interesting to me is that there's only one offensive weapon listed in the armor of God. The weapon that we have to fight hell with is the Word of God. The more you and I learn God's Word, the more effective we will be at fighting lust, depression, fear, and the list could go on forever. From this point on, view the Bible as your spiritual sword and view prayer as your wartime walkie-talkie.

DOSE OF TRUTH

For we do not wrestle against flesh and blood, but against principalities, against powers, against the rulers of the darkness of this age, against spiritual hosts of wickedness in the heavenly places. Therefore take up the whole armor of God, that you may be able to withstand in the evil day, and having done all, to stand. Stand therefore, having girded your waist with truth, having put on the breastplate of righteousness, and having shod your feet with the preparation of the gospel of peace; above all, taking the shield of faith with which you will be able to quench all the fiery darts of the wicked one, and take the helmet of salvation, and the sword of the Spirit, which is the word of God; praying always with all prayer and supplication in the Spirit, being watchful to this end with all perseverance and supplication for all the saints. —**Ephesians 6:12–18**

And a servant of the Lord must not quarrel but be gentle to all, able to teach, patient, in humility correcting those who are in opposition, if God perhaps will grant them repentance, so they may know the truth, and that they may come to their senses and escape the snare of the devil, having been taken captive by him to do his will. —**2 Timothy 2:24–26**

MAKIN' IT REAL

What outside sources influence the decisions people make?

Are there things in your life that negatively influence your attitude and actions?

What action steps do you need to take to eliminate those ungodly influences?

DAY 5: RULES VS. RELATIONSHIP

In **John 15:4–5**, Jesus gave us an incredible promise. He said, "Abide in Me, and I in you. As the branch cannot bear fruit of itself, unless it abides in the vine, neither can you, unless you abide in Me. I am the vine, you *are* the branches. He who abides in Me, and I in him, bears much fruit; for without Me you can do nothing." The promise of bearing good fruit is the result of being connected to Jesus. When we connect to Him, our lives are radically changed. For far too long we've had a limited understanding of the gospel. The Scripture says, "He (Jesus) who knew no sin, became sin for us, so that we might become the righteousness of God, in Him" (**2 Corinthians 5:21**). Jesus traded places with us. He became all that we were so that we could become all that He is. It is soooooo not about the rules anymore. The rules were given to show us how badly we needed a Savior. Even the idea that I'm strong enough to live free from failure is an idea dripping with pride. The thought that I can prove my commitment to Him by shear will power is nothing short of religious arrogance. What I really need is a life totally consumed by the Son of God. Christianity is not about decisions; it's about affections.

Jesus said eternal life is found in knowing the Father, the only true and living God, and Jesus Christ, whom the Father sent. Eternal life is found in our *relationship* with God, not our obedience to all the rules. Should we obey the rules? Of course we should! But if your walk with God is only about rules, you'll never obey them. As someone once said, "Rules without a relationship always leads to rebellion."

Many of us allow ourselves to be consumed with the cares of this life and our relationship with God is put on the back burner. Then the focus of our Christianity becomes living right—obeying the rules! I've noticed something over the years: when people focus on living right, they seldom do. These people are moody, hateful, frustrated, bitter, and a pain to be around. On the other hand, people who *love* right lift the spirit of everyone in the room. Here's the ironic thing: people who focus on *loving* right *live* right!

Our relationship with God grows as we spend more and more time in His presence. Every time you read God's Word, you are hearing the words that He has spoken for thousands of years. Listen to His words as a child would listen to his father. Each time you pray, He pulls you closer to His heart. Knowing you is His greatest joy.

Leonard Ravenhill said in his book, *Why Revival Tarries*, "No man is greater than his prayer life. . . . We have many organizers, but few agonizers, many players and payers, few prayers. The ministry of preaching is open to few, the ministry of prayer, the highest ministry of all human offices, is open to all."[6]

Seek the Lord today. Remember, it's a relationship thing, not a rule thing.

DOSE OF TRUTH

And this is eternal life, that they may know You, the only true God, and Jesus Christ whom You have sent. **—John 17:3**

Are you tired? Worn out? Burned out on religion? Come to Me. Get away with Me and you'll recover your life. I'll show you how to take a real rest. Walk with Me and work with Me—watch how I do it. Learn the unforced rhythms of grace. I won't lay anything heavy or ill-fitting on you. Keep company with Me and you'll learn to live freely and lightly. **—Matthew 11:28–30 (Message Translation)**

MAKIN' IT REAL

David King is a pastor friend of mine. Several times I heard David say, "Before we become a Christian we have a nature to do the wrong thing and a tendency to do the right thing. When we give our hearts to Christ, our nature and tendencies are reversed. We now have a nature to do the right thing and a tendency to do the wrong thing." Here's the question: why doesn't God forgive us of our sins and then remove from our lives, the ability to sin?

DAY 6: **THE DEAD FISH**

If there's a hypocrite standing between you and the church, he is closer to God than you are. It's vital that you find a community of believers to connect with on a regular basis. We weren't created to do life alone. If you're looking for the perfect church, you'll never find one. If you did find a perfect church, you would feel out of place for attending it. Christians without a church are like bees without a hive. At the close of **Psalm 23**, David writes: "Goodness and mercy shall follow me all the days of my life; and I will dwell in the house of the Lord forever."

Some people have made the comment, "I don't have to go to church to be a Christian." This may be true, but as one pastor said, "You don't have to be in the water to be a fish either." Every believer needs a local church where he or she can serve and grow. Author John Mason once said, "Life is like a tennis match—you'll lose if you can't serve." **Psalm 92:13** says, "Those who are planted in the house of the Lord shall flourish in the courts of our God."

In a healthy church, you have a support system, friends you can talk to, accountability, and the strength of numbers. If you attend a large church that offers small group environments, take advantage of the opportunity. Sometimes the loneliest place in the world is in a crowded room.

Atlanta's *11 Alive News* once stated that according to The National Institutes of Health, people who go to church regularly live 25 percent longer than those who don't. Even the secular community can see the importance of church attendance!

In the book, *Can We Do That?*, Pastor Ed Young writes: "Imagine walking up to a professional hockey player and asking him this question: 'What team do you play for?' Now suppose he answers, 'I'm a professional hockey player, but I don't play for any team.' You would think the guy had been slammed into the boards once too often. A similar scenario plays out in our society when it comes to church membership. There are many people who claim to be Christ-followers, but they are not committed to a local church."[7]

If absence makes the heart grow fonder, there are a lot of people who love the church.

DOSE OF TRUTH

Then those who gladly received his word were baptized; and that day about three thousand souls were added to them. And they continued steadfastly in the apostles' doctrine and fellowship, in the breaking of bread, and in prayers. Then fear came upon every soul, and many wonders and signs were done through the apostles. Now all who believed were together, and had all things in common, and sold their possessions and goods, and divided them among all, as anyone had need. So continuing daily with one accord in the temple, and breaking bread from house to house, they ate their food with gladness and simplicity of heart, praising God and having favor with all the people. And the Lord added to the church daily those who were being saved. —**Acts 2:41–47**

MAKIN' IT REAL

Are you currently committed to a church?

Realizing that there is no perfect church, how do you deal with hurtful situations when they arise?

What are some of the benefits of being committed to a local church?

DAY 7: **BAPTISM**

I want to take our last day together and talk to you about the importance of water baptism. First, let me assure you that there's nothing magical about the water. Whether it's creek water or tap water, water is water. It doesn't save you or wash your sins away. I explain it like this: water baptism is an outward expression of an inward conversion. It's a testimony of what's taken place in your life. The old you is buried in Christ, just like your body is buried in the water during baptism. The sin-stained person you once were, died in Christ, and you arose a new creation. **Romans 6:4** says, "Therefore we were buried with Him through baptism into death, that just as Christ was raised from the dead by the glory of the Father, even so we also should walk in newness of life."

When we are baptized, we are publicly acknowledging our faith in Jesus Christ. In **Matthew 28:16–20** and **Mark 16:16**, Jesus commands us to be baptized. Therefore, water baptism is an important step in our obedience to Christ.

The most important thing for you to remember about water baptism is that this is a wonderful opportunity for you to share with your family and friends what God has done in your life. So if you haven't been baptized, talk to your pastor, and make an appointment to do so.

I hope that you've enjoyed these past five weeks. May God continue to reveal Himself to you more and more every day.

May God's blessings be upon you,
Jason Creech

DOSE OF TRUTH

And Jesus came and spoke to them, saying, "All authority has been given to Me in heaven and on earth. Go therefore and make disciples of all the nations, baptizing them in the name of the Father and of the Son and of the Holy Spirit, teaching them to observe all things that I have commanded you, and lo, I am with you always, even to the end of the age." Amen. **—Matthew 28:18–20**

He who believes and is baptized will be saved; but he who does not believe will be condemned. **—Mark 16:16**

Buried with Him in baptism, in which you also were raised with Him through faith in the working of God, who raised Him from the dead. **—Colossians 2:12**

MAKIN' IT REAL

After you're baptized, take a moment to fill out the section below; pen down the memory of this awesome occasion.

_____

Your Name

_____

Date of Baptism

_____

Name of Participants (the minister and others involved)

_____

Location of Baptism

ENDNOTES

[1] Stephen Prothero, *God Is Not One*. (New York: Harper One, an imprint of Harper Collins Publisher, 2010), 3.

[2] Josh McDowell, *Beyond Belief*. (Wheaton: Tyndale House Publishers, 2002), 173–175.

[3] Ibid., 171–172.

[4] William and Howard Hendricks, *As Iron Sharpens Iron*. (Chicago: Moody Press, 1995), 31.

[5] Francis Frangipane, *The Three Battlegrounds*. (Cedar Rapids: Arrow Publications, 1989), 10.

[6] Leonard Ravenhill, *Why Revival Tarries*. (Bloomington: Bethany House Publishers, 1979).

[7] Ed Young and Andy Stanley, *Can We Do That?* (West Monroe: Howard Publishing Co. Inc., 2002).

ABOUT THE AUTHOR

Jason Creech became a Jesus follower at age 19. After earning his bachelor's degree in art and design, he took his first staff position at a local church in Southeastern Kentucky. He has 14 years of pastoral experience in the area of student ministry. In 2006, Jason founded Mirror-Mirror, a nonprofit organization that allowed him to bring high-energy events, college scholarships, cash prizes, and the hope found in Jesus Christ to over 58,000 public school students throughout Kentucky and abroad.

OUR FAMILY

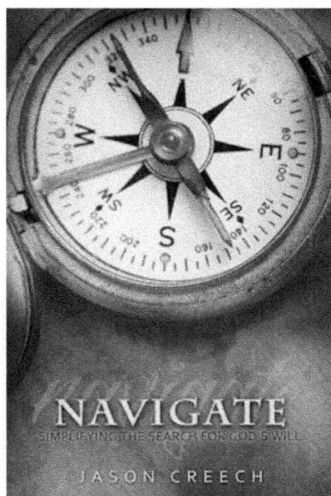

Dealing with the S-Words by Jason Creech

Rich or poor, popular or unnoticed, we're all looking for the same thing—new life. But if young people don't get things right on the inside, they will never be the happy, successful people they were created to be. Happiness and success are an inside job. This is a book about "S-Words"—the "don't go there" words—those topics that get Sunday school teachers replaced and youth pastors fired: self-esteem, significance, sex, secrets, and suicide. Dive deeply into the topics we've all wrestled with and discover what God says about life's toughest issues. ISBN 978-1-936076-70-3 PB, 978-1-936076-79-6 HB.

Navigate by Jason Creech

For most of our Christian journey we search for God's will. But what if we have it all wrong? What if we don't have to search for God's will? What if God's will searches for us?

Innovo
Publishing

Introducing *Blinders* by Kristy Shelton...

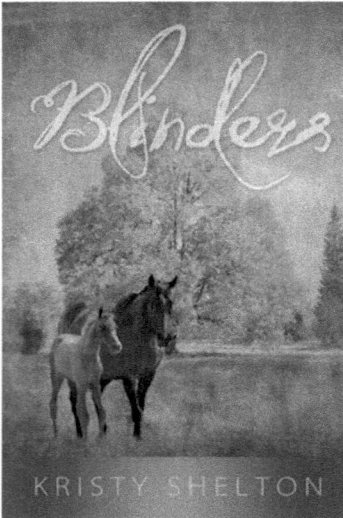

Blinders, a novel by Kristy Shelton, portrays a beautiful relationship between a former slave couple, their love for a boy who wanders onto their farm, and the redeeming forgiveness of the heavenly Father. In this inspirational novel, Eugene, an eleven-year-old boy growing up in Kentucky in 1912, is drawn to a light in the distance that compels him to run away from his abusive stepfather. He is led to the farm of Franklin and Rachel Hawkins who live in a rundown house built on top of a cave yet have magnificent thoroughbred horses grazing in their bluegrass pasture. Eugene is adopted into the family, and as he grows up, gradually discovers secrets from the past that keep Franklin and Rachel isolated on their remote farm. Eugene is severely tested when he is seized from the farm at the age of sixteen and forced into the Great War now raging in France. He embarks on a dangerous journey that will put his life and faith to the test. When he returns two years later as a man, his only hope is to give his incredible burden of guilt to the One who can save him, and allow a mother's unconditional love to help him fulfill his destiny. Available in hardback, paperback, Amazon Kindle™, Barnes & Noble Nook™, and Apple iPad™ editions.

ISBN 978-1-936076-65-9 Paperback; 978-1-936076-74-1 Hardback

Innovo
Publishing

Carson and His
Shaky Paws Grampa

Carson and His Shaky Paws Grampa, the first book in the Shaky Paws Grampa series, is a story about the relationship and love between a grandfather who has Parkinson's Disease and his seven-year-old grandson. The story is designed to help parents and grandparents comfortably talk about the initial symptoms of Parkinson's Disease and address common questions and concerns children may express. The second book in the series, *Carina and Her Bionic Grampa* (working title), is in progress and continues to portray the true story about Kirk "Shaky Paws" Hall's journey with Parkinson's Disease. The story is intended to provide a comfortable and safe setting in which parents and grandparents may talk about the more advanced symptoms of Parkinson's Disease with their children and grandchildren. *Carson and His Shaky Paws Grampa* was conceived and written by Kirk Hall and illustrated by Alison Paolini, both parents and grandparents who have been diagnosed with Parkinson's. A portion of every sale will be donated to Parkinson's research.

ISBN 978-1-936076-91-8 Hardback

ABOUT INNOVO PUBLISHING LLC

Innovo Publishing LLC is a full-service Christian publishing company serving the Christian and wholesome markets. Innovo creates, distributes, and markets quality books, eBooks, audiobooks, music, and videos through traditional and innovative publishing models and services. Innovo provides distribution, marketing, and automated order fulfillment through a network of thousands of physical and online wholesalers, retailers, bookstores, music stores, schools, and libraries worldwide. Innovo provides a unique combination of traditional publishing, co-publishing, and independent (self) publishing arrangements that allow authors, artists, and organizations to accomplish their personal, organizational, and philanthropic publishing goals. Visit Innovo Publishing's web site at www.innovopublishing.com or email Innovo at info@innovopublishing.com.

Innovo
Publishing

www.ingramcontent.com/pod-product-compliance
Lightning Source LLC
Chambersburg PA
CBHW052201090426
42741CB00010B/2360